FIGHTER
PLANES

Henry Brook

Designed by Helen Edmonds and Tom Lalonde

Illustrated by Adrian Roots and John Fox
Picture strips illustrated by Staz Johnson

Edited by Alex Frith and Jane Chisholm
Fighter planes expert: Lauren Woodard, RAF Museum, London

Contents

These startling shark designs were painted by an American unit during the Second World War. They were known as the *Flying Tigers*.

What is a fighter plane?

Fighter planes are aircraft built for combat with other aircraft. The best are hard-to-spot, fast, nimble and armed with deadly guns and missiles.

Most fighters can also attack targets on the ground, using bombs and guided missiles.

Cockpit

Nose

Two Saab Gripens in action (see page 62)

Fighter planes often fly combat missions in pairs – a lead plane supported by a wingman.

Wingman

822

Tail

Lead plane

Air intake for engine

Exhaust

Missiles and bombs are carried under the wings.

Wing

The main body of a plane is called the *fuselage*.

Taking to the skies

Only eleven years after the first recorded flight by a powered, piloted plane, the First World War broke out. Pilots began to arm their planes with weapons.

Since then, air forces around the world have competed to build faster and deadlier fighter planes.

Deadly weapons

Most modern fighters can carry different types of missiles and bombs on open parts of the plane called *hardpoints*. Missiles are rocket-powered weapons that fly; bombs are weapons dropped onto targets below.

This Eurofighter Typhoon has a total of 13 hardpoints, found under the wings and fuselage.

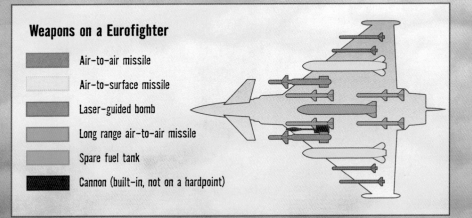

Weapons on a Eurofighter

- Air–to–air missile
- Air–to–surface missile
- Laser–guided bomb
- Long range air–to–air missile
- Spare fuel tank
- Cannon (built–in, not on a hardpoint)

Air-to-air missiles are used to attack enemy aircraft. Find out more on pages 44-45.

Air-to-surface missiles are used to attack enemy targets on land.

Some fighters carry a cannon: a weapon that fires small but deadly explosive shells.

This fighter is carrying spare fuel tanks in place of three missiles.

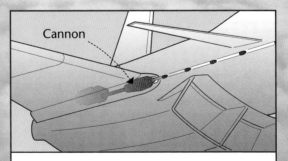

Cannon

Short range combat

A cannon hidden in the fuselage can shoot hundreds of shells in a few seconds.
On a Typhoon, the shells fly out of a hole where the right wing meets the fuselage.

Dogfights

A duel between two or more fighter planes is known as a *dogfight*.

One common tactic is for a pair of fighters to try to surround an enemy plane...

German and British fighters engage in a dogfight above the battlefields of the First World War.

1. The lead plane approaches target from above. The wingman flies beneath the target.

2. The lead plane swoops down close to the target.

3. The target is forced to make a hard turn.

German wingman

Lead plane

Wingman

Target

4. The wingman fires at the target.

German lead plane

In this scene, the lead German plane has forced one target to turn into the path of an oncoming wingman.

Fighter pilots often hide from targets by flying through clouds, and by keeping the Sun behind them.

British target

A pair of British planes chasing a German target

German target

In the cockpit

Fighter cockpits give pilots all around views of the sky and quick access to weapons and controls.

Fly-by-wire

Modern fighter pilots rely on computer and electrical systems known as *avionics* to help them fly. Avionics can turn the plane tighter and faster than any human pilot, while keeping the plane safe. This is known as *fly-by-wire*.

Cockpit controls on a Saab Gripen:

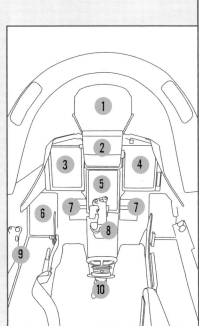

1 **HUD** – Head-Up Display screen. Find out more on pages 42-43.

2 **Control panel** – access to avionics data and communication channels.

3 **Flight data screen**

4 **Radar screen**

5 **Situation display** – map showing location of friendly and enemy aircraft.

6 **On-board computer screen**

7 **Foot pedals** – to control the rudder, which steers the plane.

8 **Control stick** – to fly the plane and fire weapons. Find out more on page 11a.

9 **Throttle** – to control the engine.

10 **Ejection seat toggle.** Find out more about ejection seats on page 68.

The birth of the fighter

When the First World War broke out in 1914, planes were used only for scouting and spying missions. But pilots wanted to shoot down enemy aircraft, too. So they fixed machine guns to their planes, creating the first fighters.

The first purpose-built fighters had a pilot and a gunner. But these planes were heavy and slow – the old one-man planes easily outflew them.

An American fighter crew in 1916

Gunner

Pilot

Roland Garros

French aviator Roland Garros was the first person to fly solo across the Mediterranean Sea. When war broke out, he took to the skies as a fighter pilot. But, like all solo pilots, he struggled to fly and shoot at the same time.

Garros in a Mourane-Soulnier monoplane

His solution was to attach a machine gun to the front of his plane so he could shoot straight ahead.

He covered his wooden propeller blades with metal strips, so bullets from his own gun would bounce off.

In April 1915, he shot down three German planes...

...but was captured when he had to make an emergency landing behind enemy lines.

Garros escaped in 1918, but by then German pilots had added a deadly new device to their fighters: a gun that could shoot through the blades of a propeller. Turn the page to find out how this worked...

Fokker's synchronizer

In 1915, Dutch aircraft designer Anton Fokker invented a device called a synchronizer for the German air force. It enabled machine guns to fire between the blades of a propeller.

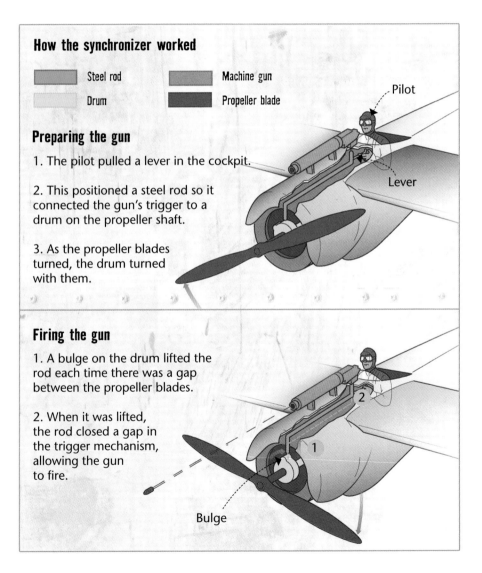

How the synchronizer worked

◼ Steel rod ◼ Machine gun
▢ Drum ◼ Propeller blade

Pilot

Preparing the gun

1. The pilot pulled a lever in the cockpit.

2. This positioned a steel rod so it connected the gun's trigger to a drum on the propeller shaft.

3. As the propeller blades turned, the drum turned with them.

Lever

Firing the gun

1. A bulge on the drum lifted the rod each time there was a gap between the propeller blades.

2. When it was lifted, the rod closed a gap in the trigger mechanism, allowing the gun to fire.

Bulge

The Fokker Scourge

Using his new device, Fokker created a deadly fleet of fighters. For months, German pilots overwhelmed French and British pilots, in a phase of the War known as the Fokker Scourge.

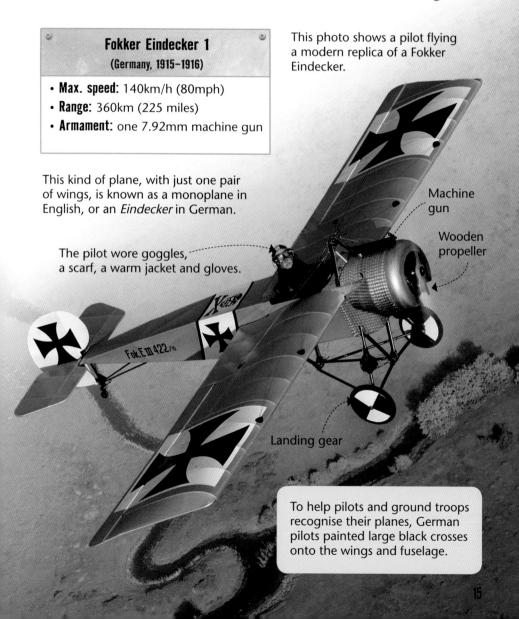

Fokker Eindecker 1
(Germany, 1915–1916)

- **Max. speed:** 140km/h (80mph)
- **Range:** 360km (225 miles)
- **Armament:** one 7.92mm machine gun

This photo shows a pilot flying a modern replica of a Fokker Eindecker.

This kind of plane, with just one pair of wings, is known as a monoplane in English, or an *Eindecker* in German.

Machine gun

Wooden propeller

The pilot wore goggles, a scarf, a warm jacket and gloves.

Landing gear

To help pilots and ground troops recognise their planes, German pilots painted large black crosses onto the wings and fuselage.

Air aces

The best pilots were given the title 'ace' after five victories in combat. Most flew in biplanes, which had two sets of wings and were more nimble than monoplanes.

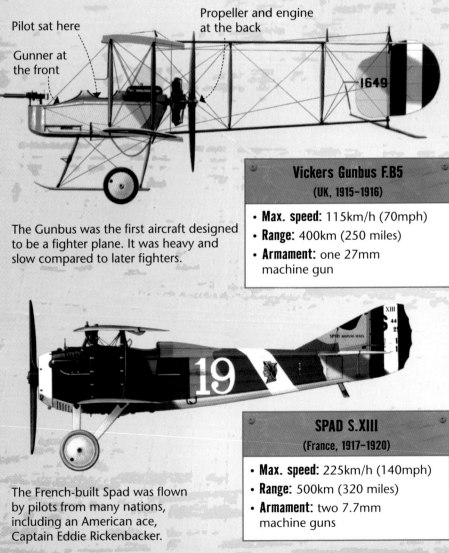

Pilot sat here

Propeller and engine at the back

Gunner at the front

1649

The Gunbus was the first aircraft designed to be a fighter plane. It was heavy and slow compared to later fighters.

Vickers Gunbus F.B5
(UK, 1915–1916)

- **Max. speed:** 115km/h (70mph)
- **Range:** 400km (250 miles)
- **Armament:** one 27mm machine gun

The French-built Spad was flown by pilots from many nations, including an American ace, Captain Eddie Rickenbacker.

SPAD S.XIII
(France, 1917–1920)

- **Max. speed:** 225km/h (140mph)
- **Range:** 500km (320 miles)
- **Armament:** two 7.7mm machine guns

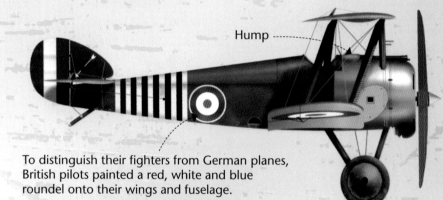

Albatros D.III
(Germany, 1916–1918)

- **Max. speed:** 175km/h (110mph)
- **Range:** 480km (300 miles)
- **Armament:** two 7.92mm machine guns

The D.III had one of the best rates of climb of the War, meaning it could fly higher into the air faster than most other planes.

Hump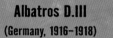

To distinguish their fighters from German planes, British pilots painted a red, white and blue roundel onto their wings and fuselage.

Sopwith Camel
(UK, 1917–1918)

- **Max. speed:** 200km/h (125mph)
- **Range:** 485km (300 miles)
- **Armament:** two 27mm machine guns; up to four bombs

The Camel took its name from a hump in the engine casing that partly covered two machine guns.

Ace of aces

German flying ace Baron Manfred von Richthofen stalked deer and wild boar as a young man, and was a successful cavalry officer.

He used his hunting skills to become the deadliest combat fighter of the War.

A fighter with three sets of wings was called a triplane.

Richthofen flew many kinds of planes, and scored over 80 combat victories in the War – more than any pilot of his time.

In 1917, he painted his Fokker DR1 fighter bright red, to match his cavalry regiment flag, and earned the nickname 'Red Baron'.

Pilots flying in the Red Baron's squadron painted their planes, too. They became known as the Flying Circus.

But Richthofen's luck ran out in April 1918. Swooping over a battlefield in a dogfight with two British Sopwith Camels, he was shot down and killed.

The troops who found his Fokker DR1 stripped it for souvenirs.

A need for speed

After the War, military leaders believed the greatest threat in the air was the long-range bomber. So they developed faster fighters that could catch and destroy raiding aircraft.

German engineers observe a prototype fighter in an enormous wind tunnel in 1940.

Huge fans blow wind over the plane to simulate high-speed flying conditions.

Find out more about this fighter, the Messerschmitt Bf109, on page 26.

The Peashooter was the first all-metal monoplane. It was also the first plane to add flaps to its wings, to slow down the plane for landing.

Boeing P26 'Peashooter'
(USA, 1932–1956)

- **Max. speed:** 377km/h (234mph)
- **Range:** 1,020km (635 miles)
- **Armament:** two 30mm machine guns

It flew faster and higher than most biplanes, but was soon far outpaced by newer fighters.

Hawker Hurricane Mk1
(UK, 1935–1941)

- **Max. speed:** 547km/h (310mph)
- **Range:** 740km (460 miles)
- **Armament:** four 20mm machine guns

The Hurricane was twice as fast as any plane in the First World War.

The Hurricane used a thin V-shaped engine that fit into a narrow fuselage.

The cockpit was covered by a canopy, protecting the pilot from high-speed air.

Landing gear retracted into the wing, which gave the plane a smooth, streamlined shape in the air.

Supermarine Spitfire

The Hurricane was fast, but the next fighter built by the British Royal Air Force (RAF), the Spitfire, was even faster. The Spitfire became the symbol of British air power during the Second World War (1939-1945).

Spitfire wings had a new shape, known as elliptical, which made the fighter a dream to fly. Pilots said the plane was as nimble as a ballerina in the air.

Canopy

Fuel tank

A metal three-blade propeller gave the Spitfire a quick rate of climb.

Engine

Cannon

Part of the wing and fuselage has been cut away so you can see inside.

During the operation known as D-Day, British pilots covered their planes with large black and white stripes, to mark them as British to distant gunners.

Radio wire to send and
receive messages

← 11m (37ft) →

9m (30ft)

Tailplane: see page 51.

W3560

Supermarine Spitfire
(UK, 1938–1952)

- **Max. speed:** 605km/h (380mph)
- **Range:** 1,840km (1,140 miles)
- **Armament:** two 20mm cannons;
  two 12.7mm machine guns

Landing gear folded
up into the wing

The Spitfire carried enough
ammunition for 15 seconds of
gunfire, longer than any previous
RAF fighter.

Aileron

Machine gun

The Battle of Britain

By the Summer of 1940, the German armed forces controlled most of Western Europe and were poised to invade Britain. The German air force (the *Luftwaffe*), had over 3,000 bombers and fighters ready to attack RAF bases and airfields.

A squadron of German Junkers Ju 87 dive bombers, or *Stukas*, flies over Britain in 1940, ready to strike.

Stukas had sirens built into their landing gear. These let out a terrifying wail during a vertical bombing dive, causing panic in the streets below.

Radar to the rescue

In the years leading up to the Second World War, British scientists learned how to track targets in the sky using radio waves. They called the process Radio Detection Finding (RDF). After the war it was widely called radar.

How radar was used

1. The RAF set up radar stations on the south coast of England. Each one sent radio waves over the English Channel.

2. Radio waves that hit enemy planes bounced back to the stations.

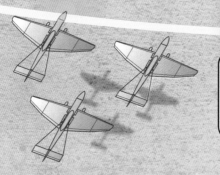

3. Technicians used the bouncing radio signals to calculate the location of enemy planes. They alerted RAF teams, who sent pilots straight into action.

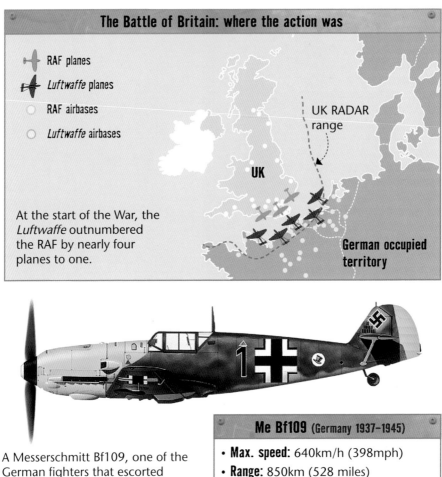

The Battle of Britain: where the action was

- RAF planes
- *Luftwaffe* planes
- RAF airbases
- *Luftwaffe* airbases

UK RADAR range

UK

At the start of the War, the *Luftwaffe* outnumbered the RAF by nearly four planes to one.

German occupied territory

A Messerschmitt Bf109, one of the German fighters that escorted bombers into British air space.

Me Bf109 (Germany 1937–1945)

- **Max. speed:** 640km/h (398mph)
- **Range:** 850km (528 miles)
- **Armament:** two machine guns; one cannon; two rockets; one bomb

Home victory

Because they fought close to their own bases, RAF pilots had longer flying time than the invaders. This advantage, along with radar and sheer bravery, meant the RAF beat back the *Luftwaffe*. The Germans abandoned daylight raids by the autumn of 1940.

Hurricane hero

On September 15, 1940, RAF pilot Sergeant Ray Holmes put his Hurricane into a collision course with a German Dornier bomber – and survived.

Dornier bomber

Holmes had already used up his ammunition shooting down two Dorniers – when he spotted a third, heading towards Buckingham Palace.

The only weapon left was the plane itself. He pushed the Hurricane into a dive and crashed his wing into the enemy aircraft, slicing off its tail.

Amazingly, the Hurricane was still in one piece, but Holmes couldn't move his control stick.

He bailed out into crowds of cheering Londoners. Meanwhile, the Dornier crashed close to Victoria Station.

Warbirds

The Second World War was the last era of great propeller-driven fighters. Here are four of the best:

Spare fuel canisters known as drop tanks meant the Zero could seek out targets at an astonishing range.

Mitsubishi A6M 'Zero'
(Japan, 1940–1945)

- **Max. speed:** 530km/h (330mph)
- **Range:** 3,100km (1,930 miles)
- **Armament:** two 20mm cannons; two 7.7mm machine guns

Drop tank ------ ➤

The Shrike could outfly and outfight early models of the RAF's Spitfire. Its weapons gave it incredible destructive power.

Focke-Wulf FW190 'Shrike'
(Germany, 1941–1945)

- **Max. speed:** 675km/h (420mph)
- **Range:** 800km (500 miles)
- **Armament:** four 20mm cannons; two 30mm machine guns

North American P-51 'Mustang'
(USA, 1942–1951)

- **Max. speed:** 700km/h (435mph)
- **Range:** 1,865km (1,160 miles)
- **Armament:** up to six 12.7mm machine guns

The Mustang was one of the fastest planes of the war. It could carry extra fuel tanks to give it the range to escort bombers deep into enemy territory.

Some Mustangs carried rocket missiles to blast tanks and other targets on the ground.

Grumman F4F 'Wildcat'
(USA, 1940–1945)

- **Max. speed:** 530km/h (330mph)
- **Range:** 1,360km (845 miles)
- **Armament:** four 12.7mm machine guns

The Wildcat was one of the toughest fighters of the war. It could withstand heavy damage from machine guns and cannon shells.

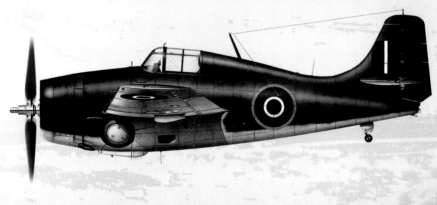

Fighters at sea

By 1941, British supply ships were under constant threat from German submarines and bomber planes. One solution was to convert ships so they carried a short, catapult-powered runway and a Hurricat – a nickname for a catapult-launched Hurricane.

The first Hurricat victory

Australian pilot Robert Everett was on duty on *HMS Maplin* when the alarm sounded: a German Condor bomber had been spotted by the ship's radar.

Everett throttled his engine and braced for take-off.

Fourteen rockets blasted Everett's Hurricat along short metal tracks, propelling it into the air.

Everett chased the Condor for nine minutes before it managed to turn and shoot at him.

Everett's Hurricat

He returned fire, and downed the Condor.

Everett lost visibility, and tried to jump from the plane, but couldn't. Instead he managed to land in the sea.

He climbed out and was rescued by a lifeboat from *HMS Maplin*.

By 1943, the British Navy had a small fleet of long ships known as escort carriers.

The biggest could carry over 20 fighters, and had flat top decks for conventional take-off and landing.

The first jet fighter

Propeller-driven fighters were getting faster throughout the War, but they were left standing by a German secret weapon that appeared in 1944 – the Messerschmitt Me262.

The Me262 was the first fighter to fly into battle using jet engines under its wings, instead of a propeller on its nose. It could fly 150km/h (90mph) faster than any RAF plane.

No propeller needed

The fuselage was smooth and streamlined, like a shark's body, to reduce drag at high speeds.

The cannons were built into the nose.

One jet engine sat under each wing.
Find out how jets work on page 52.

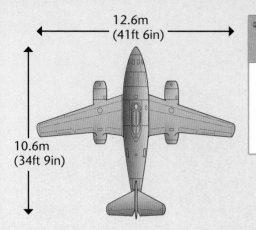

12.6m
(41ft 6in)

10.6m
(34ft 9in)

Messerschmitt Me262 'Swallow'
(Germany, 1944–1945)

- **Max. speed:** 870km/h (540mph)
- **Range:** 1,050km (652 miles)
- **Armament:** four 30mm cannons; two bombs; up to 24 rockets

The plane wasn't perfect, though. It was hard to build, dangerous to pilot and it could only fly safely for 90 minutes at a time.

By coincidence, British engineers developed a jet fighter at the same time. The Gloster Meteor took to the skies just months after the Me262.

Interceptors

Early jet fighters were used as interceptors – planes that could fly high and fast to catch and destroy bombers and a brand new threat: flying weapons.

F.1 Gloster Meteor
(UK, 1944–1954)

- **Max. speed:** 965km/h (600mph)
- **Range:** 965km (600 miles)
- **Armament:** four 20mm cannons; up to 16 rockets

Meteors were first used in combat in 1944, against a new German weapon: the V-1 flying bomb.

The V-1

V-1 flying bombs had an autopilot computer instead of a human pilot, and were designed to explode on impact.

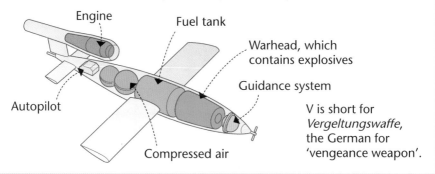

Engine

Fuel tank

Warhead, which contains explosives

Guidance system

Autopilot

Compressed air

V is short for *Vergeltungswaffe*, the German for 'vengeance weapon'.

Flipping a V-1

Almost as soon as a V-1 bomb was launched, coastal radar bases gave patrolling fighters its course and location. Interceptors had just ten minutes to stop it.

Shooting at the bomb would blow it up, but there was a risk the fighter and pilot would get caught up in the explosion.

So, interceptor pilots learned to fly close enough to the V-1 that they could disrupt the flow of air around it...

Sometimes, the wings actually touched.

...knocking it off course...

...so it fell into the sea, or exploded in an empty field. This stunt was known as *flipping*.

Going supersonic

After the end of the Second World War, fighter planes flew faster than ever. In 1947, one test pilot – American Chuck Yeager – cracked the sound barrier for the first time, using test plane Bell X-1.

XP697

Sonic boom

Sound travels at around 1,225km/h (760 mph), known as Mach 1. As a fighter accelerates to Mach 1, the airflow around it is forced into shock waves. This makes a loud crack, or *sonic boom*, that can be heard as the plane passes overhead.

In the 1960s, a Lightning fighter plane broke Mach 2 – twice the speed of sound.

English Electric Lightning
(UK, 1959–1988)

- **Max. speed:** Mach 2
- **Range:** 590km (365 miles)
- **Armament:** two 30mm cannons; two hardpoints

Faster and faster

Type of plane		In use	Speed range
Messerschmitt Me262		1942-1945	Subsonic: top speed below Mach 1
MiG15		1947-present	Transonic: top speed between Mach 0.8-1.2. Only part of the airflow around the plane is supersonic
Eurofighter		2003-present	Supersonic: top speed well above Mach 2.

Supersonic fighters

After the Second World War, pilots had to adapt to a new era in air combat using missiles and supersonic speeds. But many battles were still decided by brutal dogfights.

MiG-15
(USSR/Russia, 1947–1955)

- **Max. speed:** Mach 0.9
- **Range:** 1,325km (825 miles)
- **Armament:** one 37mm cannon; two 23mm cannons; two hardpoints

When the Korean War broke out in 1950, the Soviet Union's top-secret new MiG-15 jet fighter shocked enemy pilots with its high speed.

The MiG had swept wings, which reduced drag and kept the fighter stable even at transonic speeds.

Swept wings are angled back away from the front of the plane.

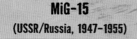

2057

Grumman F9F 'Panther'
(USA, 1947–1969)

- **Max. speed:** Mach 0.75
- **Range:** 2,100km (1,300 miles)
- **Armament:** four 20mm cannons; two bombs or six missiles

The Panther was a tough and versatile fighter. But with its straight wing and bulky design it was outmatched by the MiG-15 in the Korean War (1950-53).

MARINES
VMF-311

WL

F-86D Sabre 'Dog'
(USA, 1949–1994)

- **Max. speed:** Mach 0.9
- **Range:** 2,200km (1,320 miles)
- **Armament:** six 12.7mm machine guns; two rockets; four hardpoints

Swept wings, radar-guided gun sights and six machine guns gave the Sabre Dog enough speed and firepower to compete with a MiG-15.

Flying at high speeds puts pilots under extreme pressure, and can make them pass out. Sabre pilots were the first to be equipped with padded G-suits to prevent this. Find out more on page 67.

Dassault Mirage III
(France, 1961–1990)

- **Max. speed:** Mach 1.9
- **Range:** 1,600km (1,000 miles)
- **Armament:** two 30mm cannons; two rockets; two missiles; five hardpoints

Stealth fighters

In 1988, the United States Air Force (USAF) released photos of the F-117 Nighthawk, a stealth fighter that had been flying secret missions since 1983.

Stealth fighters are designed to hide from detection. They usually fly at night, and at very low altitudes.

F-117 Nighthawk
(USA, 1983–2008)

- **Max. speed:** Mach 0.92
- **Range:** 1,720km (1,060 miles)
- **Armament:** two hardpoints

13.2m (43ft 4in)

20m (66ft)

The Nighthawk was sometimes armed with two nuclear bombs.

The Nighthawk's startling angular shape makes radar waves bounce off it at an angle. To a radar operator, the waves appear to fold around the plane.

The wings and fuselage are also coated in special material that can absorb some radar waves.

The hardpoints are located inside the fuselage.

Ground crew preparing a Nighthawk for take-off

Nighthawk uses light-intensifying night vision equipment to map the ground and find its target.

Hiding from radar

Some surfaces on the Nighthawk have a sawtooth edge. Like the design of the fuselage, this kind of surface deflects radar waves away, instead of bouncing them back to the radar transmitter.

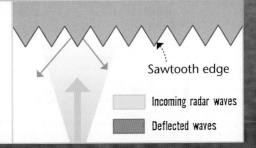

Sawtooth edge

Incoming radar waves

Deflected waves

The HUD

Fighter pilots need to fly, find targets, aim their weapons and fire
– all at the same time. To make the job easier, key information is
projected onto the plane's HUD, or Head-Up Display.

The HUD is transparent, so the pilot can
see the information and look through
the canopy at the same time.

HUD explained

1. **Airspeed indicator:** shows how fast the plane is moving in nautical miles per hour, or knots. 1 knot is about 1.9km/h (1.2mph).

2. **RWR threat indicator:** dots inside the circle show the rough location of any planes in the sky relative to the fighter.

3. **Target diamond:** shows the location of a target relative to the Velocity vector.

4. **Velocity vector:** shows the current flight path of the plane.

5. **Altitude:** shows the height of the plane above sea level.

6. **Pitch:** shows the angle of the plane relative to the horizon.

7. **Mach number:** shows how fast the plane is going relative to Mach 1.

8. **G force indicator:** shows how much force is pushing against the plane. 1G is equivalent to the pull of Earth's gravity.

9. **Distance to next waypoint:** markers so the pilot can confirm progress on a pre-planned route.

Looking through the HUD

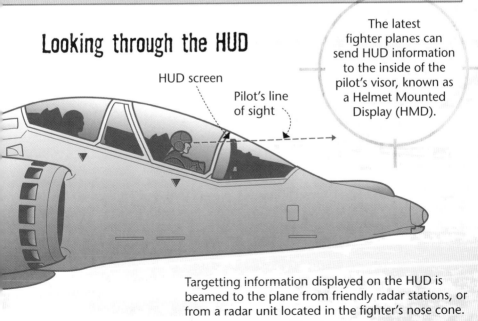

HUD screen

Pilot's line of sight

The latest fighter planes can send HUD information to the inside of the pilot's visor, known as a Helmet Mounted Display (HMD).

Targetting information displayed on the HUD is beamed to the plane from friendly radar stations, or from a radar unit located in the fighter's nose cone.

Air-to-air missiles

Fighters carry bombs and air-to-surface missiles to attack targets on land. But to attack enemy fighters, they use cannon and AAMs – air-to-air missiles.

Deadly explosion

Missiles don't have to strike the target to explode. They carry a proximity fuse that detonates the missile when sensors show the target is close. The shockwave can be powerful enough to destroy the toughest fighter planes.

Long range missiles can travel at speeds up to Mach 4, twice as fast as most fighter planes.

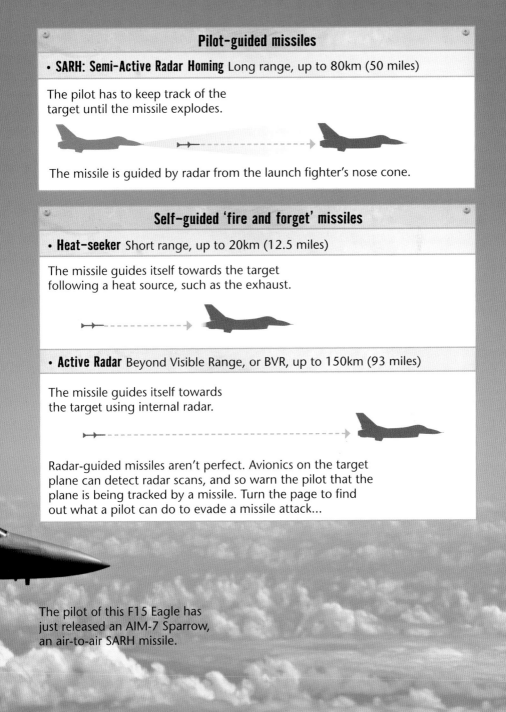

Pilot-guided missiles

• SARH: Semi-Active Radar Homing Long range, up to 80km (50 miles)

The pilot has to keep track of the
target until the missile explodes.

The missile is guided by radar from the launch fighter's nose cone.

Self-guided 'fire and forget' missiles

• Heat-seeker Short range, up to 20km (12.5 miles)

The missile guides itself towards the target
following a heat source, such as the exhaust.

• Active Radar Beyond Visible Range, or BVR, up to 150km (93 miles)

The missile guides itself towards
the target using internal radar.

Radar-guided missiles aren't perfect. Avionics on the target
plane can detect radar scans, and so warn the pilot that the
plane is being tracked by a missile. Turn the page to find
out what a pilot can do to evade a missile attack...

The pilot of this F15 Eagle has
just released an AIM-7 Sparrow,
an air-to-air SARH missile.

These SEPECAT Jaguar jet fighters zoom in formation through a valley, using the hills on either side to shield them from radar detection.

Evasive action

Special flying skills and a range of defensive weapons help pilots hide from enemy radar and missile attack.

Low to the ground

Combat pilots practice high-speed flying only 30m (100 feet) from the ground. At this height, long-range radar from enemy bases can't detect the plane, and short-range radar from missiles is confused by trees and buildings.

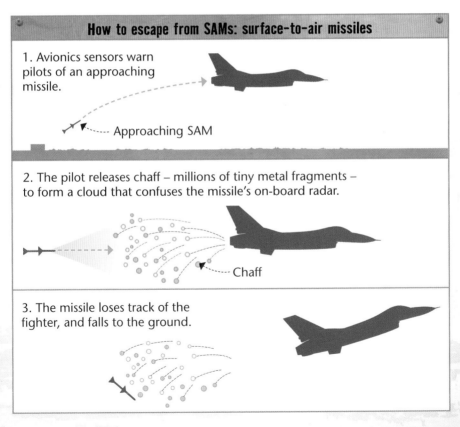

How to escape from SAMs: surface-to-air missiles

1. Avionics sensors warn pilots of an approaching missile.

Approaching SAM

2. The pilot releases chaff – millions of tiny metal fragments – to form a cloud that confuses the missile's on-board radar.

Chaff

3. The missile loses track of the fighter, and falls to the ground.

Under attack

Pilots have just seconds to respond to a missile attack from another fighter plane. Voice warnings or alarms sound in the cockpit, as the avionics system tracks the direction and speed of the incoming missile.

How to escape from AAMs: air-to-air missiles

- Pilots can fire flares from the back of their fighters. These burn brightly leaving a trail of heat behind the planes, confusing the sensors on heat-seekers.

- Skilled pilots can guide fighters into line with the sun to dazzle a heat-seeker, or hide their jet engines' heat signal by flying into thick, cold clouds.

- Cockpit ECMs (Electronic Counter Measures) produce ghost target images that can disrupt or jam a missile's radar.

Ghost images of plane

Actual plane

Radar from missile finds multiple targets.

Above the mountains of Afghanistan, the pilot of this F-15E Strike Eagle has fired off two flares.

The flares draw the attention of enemy gunners on the ground below, and away from troops that the fighter plane is supporting.

Secrets of flight

Two things make a fighter plane fly: powerful jet engines and carefully engineered wings. The engines create a force called thrust that propels the plane forward. The shape of the wings creates a force called lift, to hold it up.

How planes fly

Thrust   Lift

...and thin at the back.

Aircraft wings are thick at the front edge...

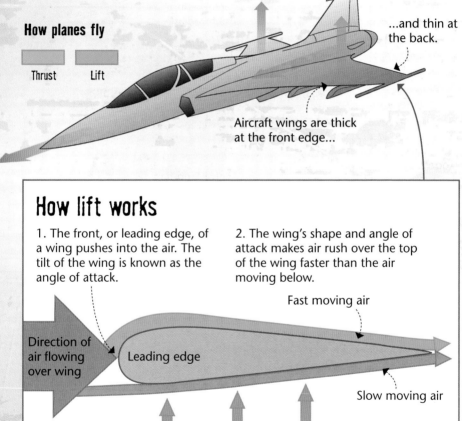

How lift works

1. The front, or leading edge, of a wing pushes into the air. The tilt of the wing is known as the angle of attack.

2. The wing's shape and angle of attack makes air rush over the top of the wing faster than the air moving below.

Fast moving air

Direction of air flowing over wing

Leading edge

Slow moving air

3. The slower moving air underneath the wing has higher air pressure than the fast moving air above. This difference in pressure creates lift.

Flying a fighter plane

Pilots control flight by adjusting parts of the wings and fuselage known as *control surfaces*.

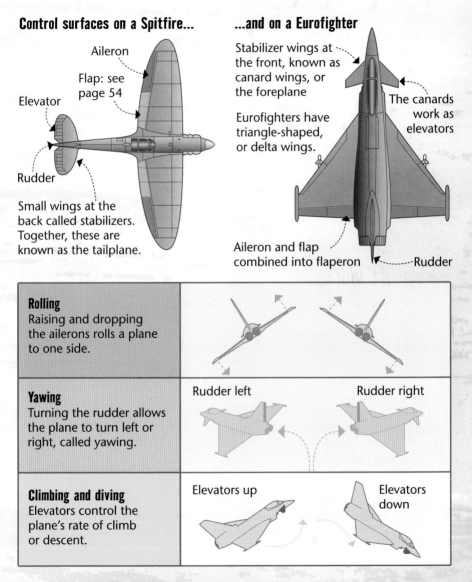

Control surfaces on a Spitfire...

Aileron

Flap: see page 54

Elevator

Rudder

Small wings at the back called stabilizers. Together, these are known as the tailplane.

...and on a Eurofighter

Stabilizer wings at the front, known as canard wings, or the foreplane

The canards work as elevators

Eurofighters have triangle-shaped, or delta wings.

Aileron and flap combined into flaperon

Rudder

Rolling Raising and dropping the ailerons rolls a plane to one side.	
Yawing Turning the rudder allows the plane to turn left or right, called yawing.	Rudder left Rudder right
Climbing and diving Elevators control the plane's rate of climb or descent.	Elevators up Elevators down

Jet power

Modern jet engines burn fuel to produce thrust, taking fighters to speeds only surpassed by spacecraft.

Engine pushes out exhaust here

The force of the exhaust at the back of the engine gives the plane its forward thrust.

Engine sucks in air through here

How a jet engine works

A jet engine works in four stages: intake, compression, combustion and exhaust.

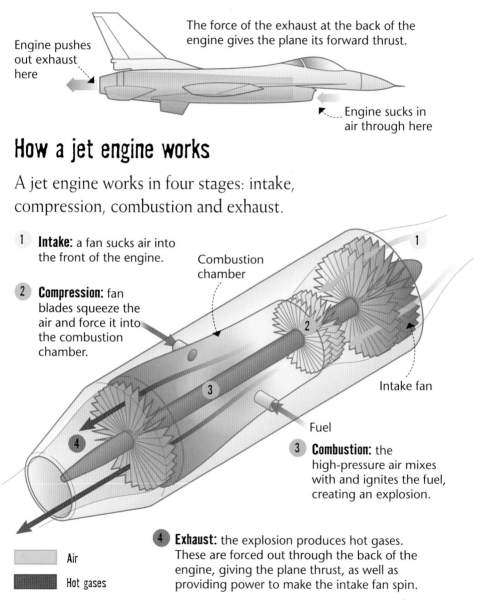

1 **Intake:** a fan sucks air into the front of the engine.

Combustion chamber

2 **Compression:** fan blades squeeze the air and force it into the combustion chamber.

Intake fan

Fuel

3 **Combustion:** the high-pressure air mixes with and ignites the fuel, creating an explosion.

4 **Exhaust:** the explosion produces hot gases. These are forced out through the back of the engine, giving the plane thrust, as well as providing power to make the intake fan spin.

Air

Hot gases

On the ground

Aircraft have to gain huge speed to generate lift under the wings. But the best modern fighters accelerate so fast they can take off from short stretches of ordinary road.

An F-16 Fighting Falcon takes off from a road.

Flaps on the trailing edge of each wing are extended to increase lift.

During take-off, the pilot fires afterburners. These inject extra fuel into the back of the engine to produce maximum thrust.

Conventional take-off

Take-off is easiest on a long runway, facing into the wind.

1. The pilot pulls the throttle, making the engine build up thrust.

2. Lift pushes the nose up when the plane is fast enough. For an F-16, that's about 225km/h (140mph).

3. After take-off, the pilot retracts, or folds back, the flaps and landing gear.

Hidden hangars

Ground crews store fighters in huge hangars that can be camouflaged or hidden underground to protect them from air attacks.

A Saab Viggen emerges from an old underground hangar, used during the Second World War for secret missions.

Overhead view of an aircraft carrier

Blast deflector protects the deck from exhaust flames

Arresting cables

Take-off

Landing

3

Catapult

Shuttle

Hold-back bar

Taking off

1 The pilot starts the engine and builds up thrust. A hold-back bar keeps the plane still.

2 The hold-back bar releases the plane, and a steam-powered catapult, or shuttle, pulls the fighter to the edge of the deck.

3 The plane reaches take-off speed in just two seconds, and flies off into the air.

Some aircraft carriers launch planes using a ramp known as a ski-jump, instead of a catapult.

Aircraft carriers

Aircraft carriers are floating air bases. They move squadrons of fighter planes across the oceans so they can operate in all corners of the globe.

Shuttle

This F/A-18C Hornet is beginning its take-off from the deck of the *USS Kitty Hawk*.

The *USS America* carrying a squadron of F-14 Tomcats and F/A-18 Hornets

Meatball

Wings folded to make room for more planes

Landing area

Landing on an aircraft carrier

1. Pilots coming in to land line their planes up by looking at a light display on deck, known as the meatball.

2. When the pilot sees the middle of a strip of amber lights glow, it means the plane is at the correct angle to land.

3. A hook on the back of the plane catches onto one of four arresting cables. A cable can bring the plane to a dead stop in seconds.

4. Once a plane hooks onto a cable, the pilot puts the engine on full thrust. This means the plane is ready to take-off immediately if the cable snaps.

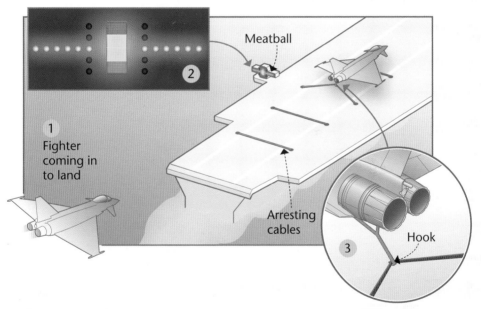

Meatball

2

1
Fighter coming in to land

Arresting cables

3

Hook

Supercarriers

The largest aircraft carriers are known as supercarriers. These enormous warships can carry up to 90 aircraft, and can land and launch a fighter every 25 seconds.

No runways

Long runways are easy targets for bombers. So, some fighters are designed to take off straight into the air. This is called vertical take-off.

How vertical take-off works

Rotating nozzles on each side of the fuselage direct thrust from the plane's engine to make it lift, hover and fly away.

1. First, nozzles point down, so the thrust pushes directly against the ground. This lifts the plane up.

Nozzle

2. As the plane lifts, the nozzles rotate until they face back.

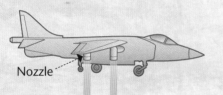

3. The thrust from the engines pushes back, making the plane fly forward.

Unlike most planes, a Harrier's wings sit above the engine.

Each wing carries its own set of wheels.

Air intakes for the engine

BAe Sea Harrier FA2
(UK, 1993–2006)

- **Max. speed:** 1,180km/h (735mph)
- **Range:** 3,600km (2,000 miles)
- **Armament:** two 30mm cannons; six hardpoints

Fuel tank

Nozzle

Nozzle

Controlling the nozzles on a Harrier is extremely difficult. Only the most skilled pilots pass the tests.

A Harrier lands on an amphibious assault vehicle. Harriers are designated as VTOL – Vertical Take Off and Landing – aircraft.

Multirole fighters

The best fighters in service today are known as multirole fighters. They're designed to fly a range of different combat missions, day or night, and in any weather.

The Sukhoi usually has a pilot and a navigator on board.

Sukhoi Su-30
(Russia, 1996–present)

- **Max. speed:** Mach 2
- **Range:** at least 3,000km (1,900 miles)
- **Armament:** one 30mm cannon; twelve hardpoints

Saab JAS 39 Gripen
(Sweden, 1996–present)

- **Max. speed:** Mach 1.8
- **Range:** 3,000km (1,860 miles)
- **Armament:** one 27mm cannon; eight hardpoints

The Gripen uses fly-by-wire technology. Find out more on page 11.

A Rafale's radar scans for incoming enemy missiles at long ranges. The fighter has advanced avionics and uses laser-guided bombs to strike ground targets.

Dassault Rafale
(France, 2000–present)

- **Max. speed:** Mach 1.8
- **Range:** at least 3,125km (1,940 miles)
- **Armament:** one 30mm cannon; fourteen hardpoints

The Lightning is one of a new generation of stealth fighters known as *superfighters.*

F-35 Lightning II
(USA, planned for service in 2016)

- **Max. speed:** Mach 1.6
- **Range:** at least 2,000km (1,400 miles)
- **Armament:** one 25mm cannon; six hardpoints

One version of the Lightning has a rotating nozzle and a fan connected to its jet exhaust, allowing it to make vertical take-offs.

Invisible fighters

The next generation of fighters will combine high-performance jets, state of the art stealth technology and intelligent avionics.

The F-22 Raptor is one of the best examples already in service.

Every part and surface of the Raptor is shaped to absorb or deflect radar tracking.

Weapons are hidden away inside internal bays.

An avionics processor sifts through data collected by the plane's radar and other sensors, and shows only the most useful information to the pilot.

Special paint and non-metal materials on the wings and fuselage reduces the fighter's heat signal, making it harder to track.

The Raptor can make sudden changes in flight direction using nozzles similar to those used by the Harrier Jumpjet. This gives the Raptor amazing agility in dogfights.

The Raptor can fly above Mach 1 using technology called Supercruise. This is much stealthier than old afterburner technology (see page 54).

External fuel tank

F-22 Raptor (USA, 2005–present)

- **Max. speed:** at least Mach 1.9
- **Range:** at least 2,960km (1,840 miles)
- **Armament:** one 30mm cannon; twelve missiles; ten bombs; four hardpoints

High flyers

Supersonic fighter pilots are a rare breed. Only the best recruits win a place at flying school and just a handful of these are chosen for jet fighter training.

To become a fighter pilot...

❶ **Apply to the Air Force or Navy to become an officer:** up to one year's training.

❷ **Pass a selection interview for flight school:** must be physically fit, and have perfect eyesight, and be the right size to fit an ejection seat.

❸ **Off to flight school:** six months training.

❹ **Pilots with the best results move onto fast jet training:** must also be extremely fit

❺ **Fast jet fighter school:** (known as TOPGUN in the USA) at least two years.

Simulators

Computer simulators test reflexes and flying skills. Pilots rely on their avionics displays to make split-second combat decisions.

Screen showing virtual landscape

G-suits and bone domes

Pilots need special suits, known as G-suits, to protect them from crushing G force during acceleration (see page 43). Helmets, known as bone domes, connect pilots to their planes in all sorts of ways.

Prototype helmet and G-suit worn by the pilot of an F-35 Lightning II

Motion sensors in the cockpit connect the helmet to the guns, so the pilot can aim by moving his head.

Tinted visor, to protect the pilot from bright sunlight

Projectors beam avionics information onto the inside of the visor, called HMD (see page 43).

Microphone for voice-activated controls

The G-suit contains pressurized pads, full of air or liquid, that squeeze the pilot's body. This stops too much blood from leaving the brain during high speed rises and turns.

Oxygen supply, so pilot can breathe at very high altitudes

Bailing out

Pilots can use rocket-powered seats to eject from the cockpit of crashing fighters. Pilots are well trained in survival techniques, whether they end up on land or at sea.

How to eject from a fighter

This fighter has been shot and the engine is on fire...

1. The pilot reaches down to pull a handle under his seat.

2. The canopy breaks off from the cockpit, and belts tighten around the pilot's legs.

3. An explosion pushes the seat up guide rails and out of the plane.

4. A motor under the seat fires up, and powers the seat away.

5. Instruments on the seat check the altitude. At the correct height, a parachute opens.

A dummy pilot is ejected from a test plane.

In this type of plane, the canopy is designed to shatter when the seat hits it.

The pilot's suit is made from fireproof and abrasion-proof material.

The entire process – from pulling the handle to opening the parachute – takes just two seconds.

Filling up

In hard-flying combat conditions, most fighters begin to run low on fuel after only a few minutes. Giant tanker planes connect to them so that they can refuel as they fly.

U.S. AIR FORCE

Probe and drogue

Some fighters, such as the Eurofighter, refuel using a 'probe and drogue' tanker.

1. This kind of tanker uncoils a long hose with an attachment at the end called a drogue.

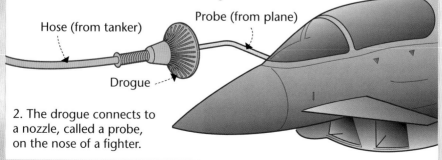

Hose (from tanker)

Probe (from plane)

Drogue

2. The drogue connects to a nozzle, called a probe, on the nose of a fighter.

This KC-135 Stratotanker refuels an F-15 Eagle during a training exercise.

This kind of tanker is known as a flying boom.

Extending boom

Fuel pipe

F-15 Eagle

Fuel tank opening

Connecting to a flying boom in the air is one of the hardest things a fighter pilot has to do.

A rigid pipe inside the boom sticks out at the end and locks onto the fuel tank of the fighter.

Future fighters

Air forces are testing Unmanned Combat Air Vehicles (UCAVs) to replace bombers and fighters over dangerous war zones. In the future, UCAVs will be flown by remote control by pilots in bases thousands of miles from the battle.

This is an artist's impression of a squadron of Dassault nEURon UCAVs.

Internal weapons bay

The absence of a cockpit allows for a sleeker design – making the nEUROn even harder to spot on radar than a stealth fighter.

Dassault nEUROn
(France, 2012–present)

- **Max. speed:** Mach 0.8
- **Range:** top secret
- **Armament:** on-board cannons; two bomb bays

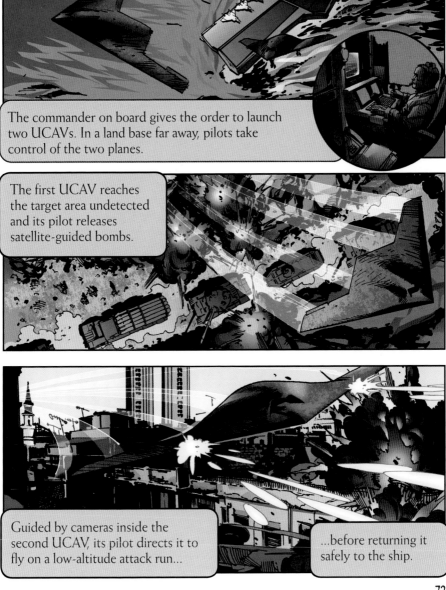

How UCAVs will work

A squadron of UCAVs waits on an aircraft carrier.

The commander on board gives the order to launch two UCAVs. In a land base far away, pilots take control of the two planes.

The first UCAV reaches the target area undetected and its pilot releases satellite-guided bombs.

Guided by cameras inside the second UCAV, its pilot directs it to fly on a low-altitude attack run...

...before returning it safely to the ship.

Fighter planes on the internet

For links to websites where you can find out more
about fighters, from the early days of the First World
War to prototype fighters of the future, go to the
Usborne Quicklinks Website at **www.usborne-quicklinks.com**
and enter the keywords **fighter planes**.

An F-22 Raptor superfighter streaks through the sky at supersonic speed.

At high speeds, sudden changes in air temperature and pressure around the plane make droplets of water condense from the air. This means viewers on the ground see a rainbow in the fighter's wake as it flies past the Sun.

Glossary

This glossary explains some of the words used in this book. If a word is written in *italic* type, it has an entry of its own.

AAM Air-to-air missile, a weapon that flies from a fighter to a target in the air.

ace A pilot who has had five or more combat victories.

afterburner A unit at the exhaust of a fighter that burns a mixture of air and fuel to produce more power.

ailerons *Control surfaces* on the wing that tilt up or down to roll and bank (turn) the plane.

altitude The height of a plane in the sky, usually measured relative to sea level or local ground level.

angle of attack The angle of the fighter's wing into the airflow. A steeper angle produces more *lift*.

avionics The electrical controls, sensors and computer around a fighter.

biplane A fighter with two sets of wings, one on top of the other.

BVR Beyond Visible Range, a designation given to missiles that can fly further than 80km (50 miles).

canard A small wing at the front of the plane that acts as a *control surface*.

cannon A gun that fires exploding shells.

chaff Tiny pieces of metal or radar-reflecting material that make it hard for enemy radar to detect a fighter.

cockpit The pilot's space in a plane.

control stick A lever fitted with buttons, used by the pilot to fly the plane and fire its weapons. Sometimes called a joystick.

control surfaces Moving panels and flaps around a plane that change its direction and speed.

delta wing A triangular wing shape that is strong and has a large surface area.

dogfight A battle between fighters.

DVI Direct Voice Input: a system that lets the pilot control flight and weapons by using speech commands.

ECM Electronic Counter Measures: a system used to escape enemy radar tracking and missile attack.

ejection seat A pilot's seat that can fly out of the cockpit in an emergency.

elevators *Control surfaces* that make a plane climb or dive.

fly-by-wire Computer systems that calculate how best to achieve the pilot's flying commands and control the plane accordingly.

fuselage The main body of a plane.

G-suit Pilot overalls that use pressure pads to maintain the flow of blood from the head and chest in extreme flying.

hardpoint A space on a fighter's wing or fuselage where weapons can be stored.

heat-seeking missile A weapon that tracks a source of heat from a target.

HUD Head-Up Display: a transparent screen that shows flight information.

landing gear The parts that support a plane on the ground. Also known as undercarriage.

lead plane The front fighter in a combat pair. *See also wingman.*

lift A force created by air pressure that keeps a flying plane in the air.

Mach number Named after an Austrian scientist, Mach 1 is the speed of sound. (Roughly 1,236km/h or 768mph).

machine gun A gun that fires bullets rapidly.

missile A rocket-powered flying weapon.

monoplane A fighter with one pair of wings.

night vision Equipment that boosts available light, and measures heat differences between objects, to help pilots see in dark or cloudy conditions.

radar A way of finding and tracking objects using radio waves.

range The distance between a gun or other weapon and its target.

also: the distance a plane can fly without refuelling.

rudder A *control surface* on the tail of a fighter used to change *yaw*.

SAM Surface-to-air missile. A weapon launched from the ground at flying targets.

streamlining The process of reducing the air resistance around a fighter by changing its shape.

supersonic Faster than the speed of sound.

swept wing A wing that angles back and away from the fighter's *fuselage*.

synchronizer A system of rods and drums that made it possible for machine guns to fire between propeller blades.

throttle The engine speed control in a cockpit.

thrust A force created by engines that pushes a plane through the sky.

transonic At speeds between *mach* 0.8-1.2, some of the airflow around a fighter is *supersonic*, and some is subsonic.

UCAV Unmanned Combat Air Vehicle, a type of fighter flown by remote control.

undercarriage *See landing gear.*

V-1 A jet-powered flying bomb used by the German army in the Second World War.

wingman The back, support fighter in a combat pair. *See also lead plane.*

yaw The left and right movement of the fighter's nose.

Index

Page numbers marked with an 'a' are found underneath the flap on that page.

Acknowledgements

Every effort has been made to trace and acknowledge ownership of copyright. If any rights have been omitted, the publishers offer to rectify this in any future editions following notification. The publishers are grateful to the following individuals and organizations for permission to reproduce material on the following pages: (t=top, b=bottom, r=right, l=left)

cover F-15E Strike Eagle © Stocktrek Images / Getty Images; **p1** Panavia Tornado © Ocean / Corbis; **p2-3** © Richard Cooke / Alamy; **p4-5** © Saab; **p6-7** © 2011 Eurofighter Typhoon; **p8-9** © Stapleton Collection / Corbis; **p10-11**; © Saab; **p12** © Bettmann / Corbis; **p15** © David J Spurdens / Getty Images; **p16-17** all © Osprey Publishing: (**tl**) Harry Dempsey, *Pusher Aces of WW1*; (**bl**) Harry Dempsey, *Lafayette Escadrille*; (**tr**) Harry Dempsey, *Albatross Aces of WW1*; (**br**) Mark Rolfe, *British and Empire Aces of WW1*; **p20** © Corbis; **p21** both © ArtTech / Aerospace Publishing; **p24** © 2011 Photo Scala, Florence / BPK; **p26** © ArtTech / Aerospace Publishing; **p28-29** (**tl**) Tom Tullis, *Imperial Japanese Navy Aces 1937-45* © Osprey Publishing; (**bl** and **tr**) both © ArtTech / Aerospace Publishing; (**br**) Chris Davey, *Wildcat Aces of WW2* © Osprey Publishing; **p32-33** © Bettmann / Corbis; **p36-37** © Popperfoto / Getty Images; **p38-39** all © ArtTech/Aerospace Publishing; **p41** courtesy of Defenseimagery.mil and Staff Sgt. Joshua Strang, U.S. Air Force; **p42** © Jamie Hunter/Aviacom; **p44-45** © Fotosearch /Photolibrary. com; **p46** © Richard Cooke / Alamy; **p48** courtesy of Defenseimagery.mil and Staff Sgt. Aaron Allmon, U.S. Air Force; **p53** © Jamie Hunter/Aviacom; **p54** courtesy of Defenseimagery.mil and Senior Airman Julianne Showalter, U.S. Air Force; **p55** courtesy of Daniel Karlsson, www.daniel-k. com; **p56-57** courtesy of Defenseimagery.mil and Mass Communication Specialist 3rd Class Patrick Heil, U.S. Navy; **p58** © Fotosearch / Photolibrary.com; **p60-61** courtesy of Defenseimagery.mil and Mass Communication Specialist 2nd Class John J. Siller, U.S. Navy; **p64-65** courtesy of Defenseimagery.mil and Senior Airman Gustavo Gonzalez, U.S. Air Force; **p66** © George Steinmetz / Science Photo Library; **p67** © Lockheed Martin; **p69** courtesy of Martin-Baker Aircraft Company Limited; **p70-71** courtesy of Defenseimagery.mil; **p72** © Dassault Aviation – M. Alleaume; **p74-75** courtesy of Bernardo Malfitano, www.airshowfan.com.

Use of photos from Defenseimagery.mil does not imply
or constitute U.S. Department of Defense endorsement.

Additional illustrations by Helen Edmonds
Digital design by John Russell
Series editor: Jane Chisholm   Series designer: Zoe Wray
Picture research by Ruth King